'. . . dreaming of
bears, or fire,
or water . . .'

THOMAS NASHE
Born 1567, Lowestoft, England
Died *c*. 1601

The Terrors of the Night first published 1594.

NASHE IN PENGUIN CLASSICS
The Unfortunate Traveller and Other Works

THOMAS NASHE

The Terrors of the Night, or
A Discourse of Apparitions

PENGUIN BOOKS

PENGUIN CLASSICS

UK | USA | Canada | Ireland | Australia
India | New Zealand | South Africa

Penguin Books is part of the Penguin Random House group of companies
whose addresses can be found at global.penguinrandomhouse.com.

This edition published in Penguin Classics 2015
002

Set in 9.5/13 pt Baskerville 10 Pro
Typeset by Jouve (UK), Milton Keynes
Printed in Great Britain by Clays Ltd, St Ives plc

A CIP catalogue record for this book is available from the British Library

ISBN: 978-0-141-39724-5

www.greenpenguin.co.uk

Glossary

bent on a head	rushing ahead
bill of parcels	catalogue
black saunt	discordant singing
bolings	bowlines
bonarobaes	courtesans
bosk	sketch
breaks with	confides in
buy wind	buy favours
cannot away with	cannot tolerate
chapmanable	saleable
chevala	'who goes there?' (*Qui va là?*)
cog	cheat (at a game)
colourable	deceitful
conceits	thoughts
conycatching	deceptive
countervailment	compensation
crepundio	empty talker
displin	disciplined
disposition	at his disposal
emayle	enamel
exornations	embellishments
extraught	derived

Glossary

foeculent	impure
gentilism	paganism
glick	jest
good big pop mouths	mouths suited to sharp yelling
incontinent	at once
a knot in a bulrush	trouble
linsey-wolsey	mixed up
lists	desires
make a coil	have a noisy conversation
make a shaft or bolt	make something definite
matachine	exotic sword dance
Molenax	Emeric Molyneux, a globe maker
Mounsier	Monsieur – the Duke of Anjou, who visited England in 1581 as a potential suitor of the Queen
pastance	food
Pater-Noster-while	the time it takes to say the Lord's Prayer
poses	catarrh
potestates	spiritual powers
Queen-Hive	Queenshithe
riding snarl	slip-knot
serena	evening rain (considered harmful)
sinkapace	lively dance
skirts and outshifts	suburbs
standish	ink-stand
surprised	captured
table	writing tablet

Tittle est amen	conclusion
Tuns	Willem Tons, a painter
welt and gard	adorn and trim
worm in his tongue	a piece of cartilage thought then to be a parasite
yare	neat
y-clepped	called

The Terrors of the Night

OR

A DISCOURSE OF APPARITIONS

A little to beguile time idly discontented, and satisfy some of my solitary friends here in the country, I have hastily undertook to write of the weary fancies of the night, wherein if I weary none with my weak fancies, I will hereafter lean harder on my pen and fetch the pedigree of my praise from the utmost of pains.

As touching the terrors of the night, they are as many as our sins. The night is the devil's Black Book, wherein he recordeth all our transgressions. Even as, when a condemned man is put into a dark dungeon, secluded from all comfort of light or company, he doth nothing but despairfully call to mind his graceless former life, and the brutish outrages and misdemeanours that have thrown him into that desolate horror; so when night in her rusty dungeon hath imprisoned our eye-sight, and that we are shut separately in our chambers from resort, the devil keepeth his audit in our sin-guilty consciences, no sense but surrenders to our memory a true bill of parcels of his detestable impieties. The table of our heart is turned to an index of iniquities, and all our thoughts are nothing but texts to condemn us.

The rest we take in our beds is such another kind of rest as the weary traveller taketh in the cool soft grass in summer, who thinking there to lie at ease and refresh his tired limbs, layeth his fainting head unawares on a loathsome nest of snakes.

Well have the poets termed night the nurse of cares, the mother of despair, the daughter of hell.

Some divines have had this conceit, that God would have made all day and no night, if it had not been to put us in mind there is a hell as well as a heaven.

Such is the peace of the subjects as is the peace of the Prince under whom they are governed. As God is entitled the Father of Light, so is the devil surnamed the Prince of Darkness, which is the night. The only peace of mind that the devil hath is despair, wherefore we that live in his nightly kingdom of darkness must needs taste some disquiet.

The raven and the dove that were sent out of Noah's Ark to discover the world after the general deluge may well be an allegory of the day and the night. The day is our good angel, the dove, that returneth to our eyes with an olive branch of peace in his mouth, presenting quiet and security to our distracted souls and consciences; the night is that ill angel the raven, which never cometh back to bring any good tidings of tranquillity: a continual messenger he is of dole and misfortune. The greatest curse almost that in the scripture is threatened is that the ravens shall pick out their eyes in the valley of death. This cursed raven, the night, pecks out men's eyes in the valley of death. It hindreth them from looking to heaven for succour, where their Redeemer dwelleth; wherefore no doubt it is a time most fatal and unhallowed. This being proved, that the devil is a special predominant planet of the night, and that our creator for our punishment hath allotted it him as his peculiar signory and kingdom, from his inveterate envy I will amplify the ugly terrors of the night. The names importing his malice, which the scripture is plentiful of, I will here omit, lest some men should think I went about to conjure. Sufficeth us to have this heedful knowledge of him, that he is an ancient malcontent, and seeketh to make any one desperate like himself. Like a cunning fowler, to this end he spreadeth his nets of temptation in the dark, that men might not see to avoid them. As the poet saith:

Quae nimis apparent retia vitat avis.
(Too open nets even simple birds do shun)

Therefore in another place (which it cannot be but the devil hath read) he counseleth thus:

Noctem peccatis et fraudibus obiice nubem.
(By night-time sin, and cloak thy fraud with clouds)

When hath the devil commonly first appeared unto any man but in the night?

3

In the time of infidelity, when spirits were so familiar with men that they called them *Dii Penates*, their household Gods or their Lares, they never sacrificed unto them till sunsetting. The Robin Goodfellows, elves, fairies, hobgoblins of our latter age, which idolatrous former days and the fantastical world of Greece y-clepped fawns, satyrs, dryads, and hamadryads, did most of their merry pranks in the night. Then ground they malt, and had hempen shirts for their labours, danced in rounds in green meadows, pinched maids in their sleep that swept not their houses clean, and led poor travellers out of their way notoriously.

It is not to be gainsaid but the devil can transform himself into an angel of light, appear in the day as well as in the night, but not in this subtle world of Christianity so usual as before. If he do, it is when men's minds are extraordinarily thrown down with discontent, or inly terrified with some horrible concealed murder or other heinous crime close smothered in secret. In the day he may smoothly in some mild shape insinuate, but in the night he takes upon himself like a tyrant. There is no thief that is half so hardy in the day as in the night; no more is the devil. A general principle it is, he that doth ill hateth the light.

This Machiavellian trick hath he in him worth the noting, that those whom he dare not united or together encounter, disjoined and divided he will one by one assail in their sleep. And even as ruptures and cramps do then most torment a man when the body with any other disease is distempered, so the devil, when with any other sickness or malady the faculties of our reason are enfeebled and distempered, will be most busy to disturb us and torment us.

In the quiet silence of the night he will be sure to surprise us, when he unfallibly knows we shall be unarmed to resist, and that there will be full auditory granted him to undermine or persuade what he lists. All that ever he can scare us with are but Seleucus' airy castles, terrible bugbear brags, and nought else, which with the least thought of faith are quite evanished and put to flight. Neither in his own nature dare he come near us, but in the name of sin and as God's executioner. Those that catch birds imitate their voices; so will he imitate the voices of God's vengeance, to bring us like birds into the net of eternal damnation.

Children, fools, sick-men or madmen, he is most familiar with, for he still delights to work upon the advantage, and to them he boldly revealeth the whole astonishing treasury of his wonders.

It will be demanded why in the likeness of one's father or mother, or kinsfolks, he oftentimes presents himself unto us.

No other reason can be given of it but this, that in those shapes which he supposeth most familiar unto us, and that we are inclined to with a natural kind of love, we will sooner harken to him than otherwise.

Should he not disguise himself in such subtle forms of affection, we would fly from him as a serpent, and eschew him with that hatred he ought to be eschewed. If any ask

5

why he is more conversant and busy in churchyards and places where men are buried than in any other places, it is to make us believe that the bodies and souls of the departed rest entirely in his possession and the peculiar power of death is resigned to his disposition. A rich man delights in nothing so much as to be uncessantly raking in his treasury, to be turning over his rusty gold every hour. The bones of the dead, the devil counts his chief treasury, and therefore is he continually raking amongst them; and the rather he doth it, that the living which hear it should be more unwilling to die, insomuch as after death their bones should take no rest.

It was said of Catiline, *Vultum gestavit in manibus*: with the turning of a hand he could turn and alter his countenance. Far more nimble and sudden is the devil in shifting his habit; his form he can change and cog as quick as thought.

What do we talk of one devil? There is not a room in any man's house but is pestered and close-packed with a camp-royal of devils. Chrisostom saith the air and earth are three parts inhabited with spirits. Hereunto the philosopher alluded when he said nature made no voidness in the whole universal; for no place (be it no bigger than a pockhole in a man's face) but is close thronged with them. Infinite millions of them will hang swarming about a worm-eaten nose.

Don Lucifer himself, their grand Capitano, asketh no better throne than a blear eye to set up his state in. Upon a hair they will sit like a nit, and overdredge a bald pate like a white scurf. The wrinkles in old witches' visages they eat out to entrench themselves in.

If in one man a whole legion of devils have been billetted, how many hundred thousand legions retain to a term in London? If I said but to a tavern, it were an infinite thing. In Westminster Hall a man can scarce breathe for them; for in every corner they hover as thick as motes in the sun.

The Druids that dwelt in the Isle of Man, which are famous for great conjurers, are reported to have been lousy with familiars. Had they but put their finger and their thumb into their neck, they could have plucked out a whole nest of them.

There be them that think every spark in a flame is a spirit, and that the worms which at sea eat through a ship are so also; which may very well be, for have not you seen one spark of fire burn a whole town and a man with a spark of lightning made blind or killed outright? It is impossible the guns should go off as they do, if there were not a spirit either in the fire or in the powder.

Now for worms: what makes a dog run mad but a worm in his tongue? And what should that worm be but a spirit? Is there any reason such small vermin as they are should devour such a vast thing as a ship, or have the teeth to gnaw through iron and wood? No, no, they are spirits, or else it were incredible.

Tullius Hostilius, who took upon him to conjure up Jove by Numa Pompilius' books, had no sense to quake and tremble at the wagging and shaking of every leaf but that he thought all leaves are full of worms, and those worms are wicked spirits.

If the bubbles in streams were well searched, I am persuaded they would be found to be little better. Hence it comes that mares, as Columella reporteth, looking their forms in the water run mad. A flea is but a little beast, yet if she were not possessed with a spirit, she could never leap and skip so as she doth. Froisard saith the Earl of Foix had a familiar that presented itself unto him in the likeness of two rushes fighting one with another. Not so much as Tewkesbury mustard but hath a spirit in it or else it would never bite so. Have we not read of a number of men that have ordinarily carried a familiar or a spirit in a ring instead of a spark of a diamond? Why, I tell ye we cannot break a crumb of bread so little as one of them will be if they list.

From this general discourse of spirits, let us digress and talk another while of their separate natures and properties.

The spirits of the fire which are the purest and perfectest are merry, pleasant, and well-inclined to wit, but nevertheless giddy and unconstant.

Those whom they possess they cause to excel in whatever they undertake. Or poets or boon companions they are, out of question.

Socrates' genius was one of this stamp, and the dove wherewith the Turks hold Mohamet their prophet to be inspired. What their names are and under whom they are governed *The Discovery of Witchcraft* hath amplified at large, wherefore I am exempted from that labour. But of the divinest quintessence of metals and of wines are many of these spirits extracted. It is almost impossible for any to be encumbered with ill spirits who is continually conversant in the excellent restorative distillations of wit and of alchemy. Those that ravenously englut themselves with gross meats and respect not the quality but the quantity of what they eat, have no affinity with these spirits of the fire.

A man that will entertain them must not pollute his body with any gross carnal copulation or inordinate beastly desires, but love pure beauty, pure virtue, and not have his affections linsey-wolsey, intermingled with lust and things worthy of liking.

As for example, if he love good poets he must not countenance ballad-makers; if he have learned physicians he must not favour horse-leeches and mountebanks. For a bad spirit and a good can never endure to dwell together.

Those spirits of the fire, however I term them comparatively good in respect of a number of bad, yet are they not simply well-inclined, for they be by nature ambitious, haughty, and proud; nor do they love virtue for itself any whit, but because they would overquell and outstrip others with the vain-glorious ostentation of it. A humour of monarchizing and nothing else it is, which makes them affect rare qualified studies. Many atheists are with these spirits inhabited.

To come to the spirits of the water, the earth and the air: they are dull phlegmatic drones, things that have much malice without any great might. Drunkards, misers and women they usually retain to. Water, you all know, breedeth a medley kind of liquor called beer; with these watery spirits they were possessed that first invented the art of brewing. A quagmire consisting of mud and sand sendeth forth the like puddly mixture.

All rheums, poses, sciaticas, dropsies and gouts are diseases of their phlegmatic engendering. Sea-faring men of what sort soever are chief entertainers of those spirits. Greedy vintners likewise give hospitality to a number of them; who, having read no more scripture than that miracle of Christ's turning water into wine in Canaan, think to do a far stranger miracle than ever he did, by turning wine into water.

Ale-houses and cooks' shady pavilions, by watery spirits are principally upholden.

The spirits of the earth are they which cry 'All bread and no drink', that love gold and a buttoned cap above heaven. The worth in nought they respect, but the weight; good wits they naturally hate, insomuch as the element of fire, their progenitor, is a waste-good and a consumer. If with their earth-ploughing snouts they can turn up a pearl out of a dunghill, it is all they desire. Witches have many of these spirits and kill kine with them. The giants and chieftains of those spirits are powerful sometimes to bring men to their ends, but not a jot of good can they do for their lives.

Soldiers with these terrestial spirits participate part of their essence; for nothing but iron and gold, which are earth's excrements, they delight in. Besides, in another kind they may be said to participate with them, insomuch as they confirm them in their fury and congeal their minds with a bloody resolution. Spirits of the earth they were that entered into the herd of swine in the gospel. There is no city merchant or country purchaser, but is haunted with a whole host of these spirits of the earth. The Indies is their metropolitan realm of abode.

As for the spirits of the air, which have no other visible bodies or form, but such as by the unconstant glimmering of our eyes is begotten, they are in truth all show and no substance, deluders of our imagination and naught else. Carpet knights, politic statesmen, women and children they most converse with. Carpet knights they inspire with a humour of setting big looks on it, being the basest cowards under heaven, covering an ape's heart with a lion's case, and making false alarums when they mean nothing but a may-game. Politic statesmen they privily incite to blear the world's eyes with clouds of common-wealth pretences, to broach any enmity or ambitious humour of their own under a title of their country's pre-servation; to make it fair or foul when they list, to procure popularity, or induce a preamble to some mighty piece of prowling, to stir up tempests round about, and replen-ish heaven with prodigies and wonders, the more to ratify their avaricious religion. Women they underhand instruct to pounce and bolster out their brawn-fallen deformities, to new parboil with painting their rake-lean withered visages, to set up flax shops on their foreheads when all their own hair is dead and rotten, to stick their gums round with comfits when they have not a tooth left in their heads to help them to chide withal.

Children they seduce with garish objects, and toyish babies, abusing them many years with slight vanities. So that you see all their whole influence is but thin overcast vapours, flying clouds dispersed with the least wind of wit or understanding.

None of these spirits of the air or the fire have so much predominance in the night as the spirits of the earth and the water; for they feeding on foggy-brained melancholy engender thereof many uncouth terrible monsters. Thus much observe by the way, that the grossest part of our blood is the melancholy humour, which in the spleen congealed whose office is to disperse it, with his thick steaming fenny vapours casteth a mist over the spirit and clean bemasketh the fantasy.

And even as slime and dirt in a standing puddle engender toads and frogs and many other unsightly creatures, so this slimy melancholy humour, still still thickening as it stands still, engendreth many misshapen objects in our imaginations. Sundry times we behold whole armies of men skirmishing in the air: dragons, wild beasts, bloody streamers, blazing comets, fiery streaks, with other apparitions innumberable. Whence have all these their conglomerate matter but from fuming meteors that arise from the earth? So from the fuming melancholy of our spleen mounteth that hot matter into the higher region of the brain, whereof many fearful visions are framed. Our reason even like drunken fumes it displaceth and intoxicates, and yields up our intellective apprehension to be mocked and trodden under foot by every false object or counterfeit noise that comes near it. Herein specially consisteth our senses' defect and abuse, that those organical parts, which to the mind are ordained ambassadors, do not their message as they ought, but, by some misdiet or misgovernment being distempered, fail in their report and deliver up nothing but lies and fables.

Such is our brain oppressed with melancholy, as is a clock tied down with too heavy weights or plummets; which as it cannot choose but monstrously go a-square or not go at all, so must our brains of necessity be either monstrously distracted or utterly destroyed thereby.

Lightly this extremity of melancholy never cometh, but before some notable sickness; it faring with our brains as with bees, who, as they exceedingly toil and turmoil before a storm or change of weather, so do they beat and toil and are infinitely confused before sickness.

Of the effects of melancholy I need not dilate, or discourse how many encumbered with it have thought themselves birds and beasts, with feathers and horns and hides; others, that they have been turned into glass; others, that if they should make water they should drown all the world; others, that they can never bleed enough.

Physicians in their circuit every day meet with far more

ridiculous experience. Only it shall suffice a little by the way to handle one special effect of it, which is dreams.

A dream is nothing else but a bubbling scum or froth of the fancy, which the day hath left undigested; or an after-feast made of the fragments of idle imaginations.

How many sorts there be of them no man can rightly set down, since it scarce hath been heard there were ever two men that dreamed alike. Divers have written diversely of their causes, but the best reason among them all that I could ever pick out was this: that as an arrow which is shot out of a bow is sent forth many times with such force that it flieth far beyond the mark whereat it was aimed, so our thoughts, intensively fixed all the daytime upon a mark we are to hit, are now and then overdrawn with such force that they fly beyond the mark of the day into the confines of the night. There is no man put to any torment, but quaketh and trembleth a great while after the executioner hath withdrawn his hand from him. In the daytime we torment our thoughts and imaginations with sundry cares and devices; all the night-time they quake and tremble after the terror of their late suffering, and still continue thinking of the perplexities they have endured. To nothing more aptly can I compare the working of our brains after we have unyoked and gone to bed than to the glimmering and dazzling of a man's eyes when he comes newly out of the bright sun into the dark shadow.

Even as one's eyes glimmer and dazzle when they are withdrawn out of the light into darkness, so are our thoughts troubled and vexed when they are retired from labour to ease, and from skirmishing to surgery.

You must give a wounded man leave to groan while he is in dressing. Dreaming is no other than groaning, while sleep our surgeon hath us in cure.

He that dreams merrily is like a boy new breeched, who leaps and danceth for joy his pain is passed. But long that joy stays not with him, for presently after, his master, the day, seeing him so jocund and pleasant, comes and does as much for him again, whereby his hell is renewed.

No such figure as the first chaos whereout the world was extraught, as our dreams in the night. In them all states, all sexes, all places, are confounded and meet together.

Our cogitations run on heaps like men to part a fray where every one strikes his next fellow. From one place to another without consultation they leap, like rebels bent on a head. Soldiers just up and down they imitate at the sack of a city, which spare neither age nor beauty: the young, the old, trees, steeples and mountains, they confound in one gallimaufry.

Of those things which are most known to us, some of us that have moist brains make to ourselves images of memory. On those images of memory whereon we build in the day, comes some superfluous humour of ours, like a jackanapes, in the night, and erects a puppet stage or some such ridiculous idle childish invention.

A dream is nothing else but the echo of our conceits in the day.

But otherwhile it falls out that one echo borrows of another; so our dreams, the echoes of the day, borrow of any noise we hear in the night.

As for example: if in the dead of the night there be any rumbling, knocking or disturbance near us, we straight dream of wars or of thunder. If a dog howl, we suppose we are transported into hell, where we hear the complaint of damned ghosts. If our heads lie double or uneasy, we imagine we uphold all heaven with our shoulders, like Atlas. If we be troubled with too many clothes, then we suppose the night mare rides us.

I knew one that was cramped, and he dreamed that he was torn in pieces with wild horses; and another, that having a black sant brought to his bedside at midnight, dreamt he was bidden to dinner at Ironmongers' Hall.

Any meat that in the daytime we eat against our stomachs, begetteth a dismal dream. Discontent also in dreams hath no little predominance; for even as from water that is troubled, the mud dispersingly ascendeth from the bottom to the top, so when our blood is chased, disquieted and troubled all the light imperfect humours of our body ascend like mud up aloft into the head.

The clearest spring a little touched is creased with a thousand circles; as those momentary circles for all the world, such are our dreams.

When all is said, melancholy is the mother of dreams, and of all terrors of the night whatsoever. Let it but affirm it hath seen a spirit, though it be but the moonshine on the wall, the best reason we have cannot infringe it.

Of this melancholy there be two sorts: one that, digested by our liver, swimmeth like oil above water and that is rightly termed women's melancholy, which lasteth but for an hour and is, as it were, but a copy of their countenance; the other sinketh down to the bottom like the lees of the wine, and that corrupteth all the blood and is the causer of lunacy. Well-moderated recreations are the medicine to both: surfeit or excessive study the causers of either.

There were gates in Rome out of which nothing was carried but dust and dung, and men to execution; so, many of the gates of our senses serve for nothing but to convey our excremental vapours and affrighting deadly dreams, that are worse than executioners unto us.

Ah, woe be to the solitary man that hath his sins continually about him, that hath no withdrawing place from the devil and his temptations.

Much I wonder how treason and murder dispense with the darkness of the night, how they can shrive themselves to it, and not rave and die. Methinks they should imagine that hell embraceth them round, when she overspreads them with her black pitchy mantle.

Dreams to none are so fearful, as to those whose accusing private guilt expects mischief every hour for their merit. Wonderful superstitious are such persons in observing every accident that befalls them; and that their superstition is as good as an hundred furies to torment them. Never in this world shall he enjoy one quiet day, that once hath given himself over to be her slave. His ears cannot glow, his nose itch, or his eyes smart, but his destiny stands upon her trial, and till she be acquitted or condemned he is miserable.

A cricket or a raven keep him forty times in more awe than God or the devil.

If he chance to kill a spider, he hath suppressed an enemy; if a spinner creep upon him, he shall have gold rain down from heaven. If his nose bleed, some of his kinsfolks is dead; if the salt fall right against him, all the stars cannot save him from some immediate misfortune.

The first witch was Proserpine, and she dwelt half in heaven and half in hell; half-witches are they that pretending any religion, meddle half with God and half with the devil. Meddling with the devil I call it, when ceremonies are observed which have no ground from divinity.

In another kind, witches may be said to meddle half with GOD and half with the Devil, because in their exorcisms, they use half scripture and half blasphemy.

The greatest and notablest heathen sorcerers that ever were, in all their hellish adjurations used the name of the one true and everliving God; but such a number of damned potestates they joined with him, that it might seem the stars had darkened the sun, or the moon was eclipsed by candlelight.

Of all countries under the sky, Persia was most addicted unto dreams. Darius, King of the Medes and Persians, before his fatal discomfiture, dreamt he saw an estrich with a winged crown overrunning the earth and devouring his jewel-coffer as if it had been an ordinary piece of iron. The jewel-coffer was by Alexander surprised, and afterward Homer's works in it carried before him, even as the mace or purse is customably carried before our Lord Chancellor.

Hannibal dreamed a little before his death that he was drowned in the poisonous Lake Asphaltites, when it was presently his hap within some days' distance, to seek his fate by the same means in a vault under the earth.

In India, the women very often conceive by devils in their sleep.

In Iceland, as I have read and heard, spirits in the likeness of one's father or mother after they are deceased do converse with them as naturally as if they were living.

Other spirits like rogues they have among them, destitute of all dwelling and habitation, and they chillingly complain if a constable ask them *Chevala* in the night, that they are going unto Mount Hecla to warm them.

That Mount Hecla a number conclude to be hell mouth; for near unto it are heard such yellings and groans as Ixion, Titius, Sisyphus and Tantalus blowing all in one trumpet of distress could never conjoined bellow forth.

Bondmen in Turkey or in Spain are not so ordinarily sold as witches sell familiars there. Far cheaper may you buy a wind amongst them than you can buy wind or fair words in the Court. Three knots in a thread, or an odd grandam's blessing in the corner of a napkin will carry you all the world over.

We when we frown knit our brows, but let a wizard there knit a noose or a riding snarl on his beard, and it is hail, storm and tempest a month after.

More might be spoken of the prodigies this country sends forth, if it were not too much erring from my scope. Whole islands they have of ice, on which they build and traffic as on the mainland.

Admirable, above the rest, are the incomprehensible wonders of the bottomless Lake Vether, over which no fowl flies but is frozen to death, nor any man passeth but he is senselessly benumbed like a statue of marble.

All the inhabitants round about it are deafened with the hideous roaring of his waters when the winter breaketh up, and the ice in his dissolving gives a terrible crack like to thunder, whenas out of the midst of it, as out of Mont-Gibell, a sulphureous stinking smoke issues, that wellnigh poisons the whole country.

A poison light on it, how come I to digress to such a dull, lenten, northern clime, where there is nothing but stock-fish, whetstones and cods' heads? Yet now I remember me: I have not lost my way so much as I thought, for my theme is the terrors of the night, and Iceland is one of the chief kingdoms of the night, they having scarce so much day there as will serve a child to ask his father blessing. Marry, with one commodity they are blest: they have ale that they carry in their pockets like glue, and ever when they would drink, they set it on fire and melt it.

It is reported that the Pope long since gave them a dispensation to receive the sacrament in ale, insomuch as, for their uncessant frosts there, no wine but was turned to red emayle as soon as ever it came amongst them.

Farewell, frost: as much to say as 'Farewell, Iceland', for I have no more to say to thee.

I care not much if I dream yet a little more, and to say the troth, all this whole tractate is but a dream, for my wits are not half awaked in it; and yet no golden dream, but a leaden dream is it, for in a leaden standish I stand fishing all day, but have none of Saint Peter's luck to bring a fish to the hook that carries any silver in the mouth. And yet there be of them that carry silver in the mouth too, but none in the hand; that is to say, are very bountiful and honourable in their words, but (except it be to swear indeed) no other good deeds come from them.

Filthy Italianate compliment-mongers they are who would fain be counted the Court's *Gloriosos*, and the refined judges of wit when if their wardrobes and the withered bladders of their brains were well searched, they have nothing but a few moth-eaten cod-piece suits, made against the coming of Mounsier, in the one, and a few scraps of outlandish proverbs in the other, and these alone do buckler them from the name of beggars and idiots. Otherwhile perhaps they may keep a coil with the spirit of Tasso, and then they fold their arms like braggarts, writhe their necks *alla Neapolitano*, and turn up their eye-balls like men entranced.

Come, come, I am entranced from my text, I wote well, and talk idly in my sleep longer than I should. Those that will harken any more after dreams, I refer them to Artimidorus, Synesius, and Cardan, with many others which only I have heard by their names, but I thank God had never the plodding patience to read, for if they be no better than some of them I have perused, every weatherwise old wife might write better.

What sense is there that the yoke of an egg should signify gold, or dreaming of bears, or fire, or water, debate and anger, that everything must be interpreted backward as witches say their *Pater Noster*, good being the character of bad, and bad of good?

As well we may calculate from every accident in the day, and not go about any business in the morning till we have seen on which hand the crow sits.

'Oh Lord,' I have heard many a wise gentlewoman say, 'I am so merry and have laughed so heartily, that I am sure ere long to be crossed with some sad tidings or other' – all one as if men coming from a play should conclude, 'Well, we have seen a comedy today, and therefore there cannot choose but be a tragedy tomorrow.'

I do not deny but after extremity of mirth follow many sad accidents, but yet those sad accidents, in my opinion, we merely pluck on with the fear of coming mischief, and those means we in policy most use to prevent it soonest enwrap us in it; and that was Satan's trick in the old world of gentilism to bring to pass all his blind prophecies.

Could any men set down certain rules of expounding of dreams, and that their rules were general, holding in all as well as in some, I would begin a little to list to them; but commonly that which is portentive in a king is but a frivolous fancy in a beggar, and let him dream of angels, eagles, lions, griffons, dragons never so, all the augury under heaven will not allot him so much as a good alms.

Some will object unto me for the certainty of dreams, the dreams of Cyrus, Cambyses, Pompey, Caesar, Darius and Alexander. For those I answer that they were rather visions than dreams, extraordinarily sent from heaven to foreshow the translation of monarchies.

The Greek and Roman histories are full of them, and such a stir they keep with their augurers and soothsayers, how they foretold long before by dreams and beasts' and birds' entrails the loss of such a battle, the death of such a captain or emperor, when, false knaves, they were all as prophet Calchas, pernicious traitors to their country and them that put them in trust, and were many times hired by the adverse part to dishearten and discourage their masters by such conycatching riddles as might in truth be turned any way.

An easy matter was it for them to prognosticate treasons and conspiracies, in which they were underhand inlinked themselves; and however the world went, it was a good policy for them to save their heads by the shift, for if the treasons chanced afterwards to come to light, it would not be suspected they were practisers in them, insomuch as they revealed them; or if they should by their confederates be appealed as practisers, yet might they plead and pretend it was done but of spite and malice to supplant them for so bewraying and laying open their intents.

This trick they had with them besides, that never till the very instant that any treason was to be put in execution, and it was so near at hand that the Prince had no time to prevent it, would they speak one word of it, or offer to disclose it. Yea, and even then such unfit seasons for their colourable discovery would they pick forth, as they would be sure he should have no leisure to attend it.

But you will ask why at all as then, they should step forth to detect it. Marry, to clear themselves to his successors, that there might be no revenge prosecuted on their lives.

So did Spurina, the great astrologer; even as Caesar in the midst of all his business was going hastily to the Senate House, he popped a bill in his hand of Brutus' and Cassius' conspiracy, and all the names of those that were colleagued with them.

Well he might have thought that in such haste by the highway side, he would not stay to peruse any schedules, and well he knew and was ascertained that as soon as ever he came into the Capitol the bloody deed was to be accomplished.

Shall I impart unto you a rare secrecy how these great famous conjurors and cunning men ascend by degrees to foretell secrets as they do? First and foremost they are men which have had some little sprinkling of grammar learning in their youth, or at least I will allow them to have been surgeons' or apothecaries' prentices; these, I say, having run through their thrift at the elbows, and riotously amongst harlots and make-shifts spent the annuity of halfpenny ale that was left them, fall a-beating their brains how to botch up an easy gainful trade, and set a new nap on an old occupation.

Hereupon presently they rake some dunghill for a few dirty boxes and plasters, and of toasted cheese and candles' ends temper up a few ointments and syrups; which having done, far north or into some such rude simple country they get them and set up.

Scarce one month have they stayed there, but what with their vaunting and prating, and speaking fustian instead of Greek, all the shires round about do ring with their fame; and then they begin to get them a library of three or four old rusty manuscript books, which they themselves nor any else can read, and furnish their shops with a thousand *quid pro quos*, that would choke any horse, besides some waste trinkets in their chambers hung up, which may make the world half in jealousy they can conjure.

They will evermore talk doubtfully, as if there were more in them than they meant to make public, or was appliable to every common man's capacity; when, God be their rightful judge, they utter all that they know and a great deal more.

To knit up their knaveries in short (which in sooth is the hangman's office and none's else), having picked up their crumbs thus prettily well in the country, they draw after a time a little nearer and nearer to London; and at length into London they filch themselves privily – but how? Not in the heart of the City will they presume at first dash to hang out their rat-banners, but in the skirts and outshifts steal out a sign over a cobbler's stall, like aqua vitae sellers, and stocking menders.

Many poor people they win to believe in them, who have not a barrelled herring or a piece of poor-john that looks ill on it, but they will bring the water that he was steeped in unto them in an urinal, and crave their judgement whether he be rotten, or merchant and chapmanable, or no. The bruit of their cunning thus travelling from ale-house to ale-house at length is transported in the great hilts of one or other country serving-man's sword to some good tavern or ordinary; where it is no sooner alive, but it is greedily snatched up by some dappert Monsieur Diego, who lives by telling of news, and false dice, and it may be hath a pretty insight into the cards also, together with a little skill in his Jacob's staff and his compasses, being able at all times to discover a new passage to Virginia.

This needy gallant, with the qualities aforesaid, straight trudgeth to some nobleman's to dinner, and there enlargeth the rumour of this new physician, comments upon every glass and vial that he hath, raleth on our Galenists, and calls them dull gardeners and hay-makers in a man's belly, compares them to dogs, who when they are sick eat grass, and says they are no better than pack or malt-horses, who, if a man should knock out their brains, will not go out of the beaten highway; whereas his horse-leach will leap over the hedge and ditch of a thousand Dioscorides and Hippocrates, and give a man twenty poisons in one, but he would restore him to perfect health. With this strange tale the nobleman inflamed desires to be acquainted with him; what does me he, but goes immediately and breaks with this mountebank, telling him if he will divide his gains with him, he will bring him in custom with such and such states, and he shall be countenanced in the Court as he would desire. The hungry druggier, ambitious after preferment, agrees to anything, and to Court he goes; where, being come to interview, he speaks nothing but broken English like a French doctor, pretending to have forgotten his natural tongue by travel, when he hath never been farther than either the Low Countries or Ireland, enforced thither to fly either for getting a maid with child, or marrying two wives. Sufficeth he set a good face on it, and will swear he can extract a better balsamum out of a chip than the balm of Judea; yea, all receipts and authors you can name he syllogizeth of, and makes a pish at, in comparison of them he hath seen and read; whose names if you ask, he claps you in the mouth with half-a-dozen spruce titles, never till he invented them heard of by any Christian. But this is most certain: if he be of any sect, he is a metal-brewing Paracelsian, having not passed one or two probatums for all diseases. Put case he be called to practise, he excuseth it by great cures he hath in hand; and will not encounter an infirmity but in the declining, that his credit may be more authentical, or else when by some secret intelligence he is throughly instructed of the whole process of his unrecoverable extremity, he comes gravely marching like a judge, and gives peremptory sentence of death; whereby he is accounted a prophet of deep prescience.

But how he comes to be the devil's secretary, all this long tale unrips not.

In secret be it spoken, he is not so great with the devil as you take it. It may be they are near akin, but yet you have many kindred that will do nothing for one another; no more will the devil for him, except it be to damn him.

This is the *Tittle est amen* of it: that when he waxeth stale, and all his pisspots are cracked and will no longer hold water, he sets up a conjuring school and undertakes to play the bawd to Lady Fortune.

Not a thief or a cut-purse, but a man that he keeps doth associate with, and is of their fraternity; only that his master when anything is stolen may tell who it is that hath it. In petty trifles having gotten some credit, great peers entertain him for one of their privy council, and if they have any dangerous enterprise in hand, they consult with him about success.

All malcontents intending any invasive violence against their Prince and country run headlong to his oracle.

Contrary factions enbosom unto him their inwardest com-plots, whilst he like a crafty jack-a-both-sides, as if he had a spirit still at his elbow, reciprocally embowelleth to the one what the other goes about, receiving no intelligence from any familiar, but their own mouths. I assure you most of our chief noted augurers and soothsayers in England at this day, by no other art but this gain their reputation.

They may very well pick men's purses, like the unskil-fuller cozening kind of alchemists, with their artificial and ceremonial magic, but no effect shall they achieve thereby, though they would hang themselves. The reason is, the devil of late is grown a puritan and cannot away with any ceremonies; he sees all princes have left off their states, and he leaves off his state too and will not be invo-cated with such solemnity as he was wont.

Private and disguised, he passeth to and fro, and is in a thousand places in an hour.

Fair words cannot any longer beguile him, for not a cue of courtesy will he do any man, except it be upon a flat bill of sale, and so he chaffers with wizards and witches every hour.

Now the world is almost at an end, he hath left form and is all for matter; and like an embroiderer or a tailor, he maketh haste of work against a good time, which is the Day of Judgment. Therefore, you goodmen exorcisers, his old acquaintance, must pardon him, though (as here-tofore) he stay not to dwell upon compliments.

In diebus illis [once upon a time] when Corineus and

Gogmagog were little boys, I will not gainsay but he was wont to jest and sport with country people, and play the Goodfellow amongst kitchen-wenches, sitting in an evening by the fireside making of possets, and come a-wooing to them in the likeness of a cooper, or a curmudgeonly purchaser; and sometimes he would dress himself like a barber, and wash and shave all those that lay in such a chamber. Otherwhile, like a stale cutter of Queen-hive, he would justle men in their own houses, pluck them out of bed by the heels, and dance in chains from one chamber to another. Now there is no goodness in him but miserableness and covetousness.

Sooner he will pare his nails cleanly than cause a man to dream of a pot of gold, or a money-bag that is hid in the eaves of a thatched house.

(Here is to be noted, that it is a blessed thing but to dream of gold, though a man never have it.)

Such a dream is not altogether ridiculous or impertinent, for it keeps flesh and blood from despair. All other are but as dust we raise by our steps, which awhile mounteth aloft and annoyeth our eye-sight, but presently disperseth and vanisheth.

Señor Satan, when he was a young stripling and had not yet gotten perfect audacity to set upon us in the day-time, was a sly politician in dreams; but those days are gone with him, and now that he is thoroughly steeled in his scutchery, he plays above-board boldly, and sweeps more stakes than ever he did before.

I have rid a false gallop these three or four pages. Now I care not if I breathe me and walk soberly and demurely half-a-dozen turns, like a grave citizen going about to take the air.

To make a shaft or a bolt of this drumbling subject of dreams, from whence I have been tossed off and on I know not how, this is my definitive verdict: that one may as well by the smoke that comes out of a kitchen guess what meat is there a-broach, as by paraphrasing on smoky dreams preominate of future events. Thus far notwithstanding I'll go with them: physicians by dreams may better discern the distemperature of their pale clients, than either by urine or ordure.

He that is inclining to a burning fever shall dream of frays, lightning and thunder, of skirmishing with the devil and a hundred such-like. He that is spiced with the gout or the dropsy frequently dreameth of fetters and manacles and being put on the bilbows, that his legs are turned to marble or adamant, and his feet, like the giants that scaled heaven, kept under with Mount Ossa and Pelion and erst-while that they are fast locked in quagmires. I have heard aged mumping beldams as they sat warming their knees over a coal scratch over the argument very curiously, and they would bid young folks beware on what day they pared their nails, tell what luck everyone should have by the day of the week he was born on; show how many years a man should live by the number of wrinkles on his forehead, and stand descanting not a little of the difference in fortune when they are turned upward and when they are bent downward; 'him that had a wart on his chin', they would confidently ascertain he should 'have no need of any of his kin'; marry, they would likewise distinguish between the standing of the wart on the right side and on the left. When I was a little child, I was a great auditor of theirs, and had all their witchcrafts at my fingers' ends, as perfect as good-morrow and good-even.

Of the signification of dreams, whole catalogues could I recite of theirs, which here there is no room for; but for a glance to this purpose this I remember they would very soberly affirm, that if one at supper eat birds, he should dream of flying; if fish, of swimming; if venison, of hunting, and so for the rest; as though those birds, fish, and venison being dead and digested did fly, swim and hold their chase in their brains; or the solution of our dreams should be nought else but to express what meats we ate over-night.

From the unequal and repugnant mixture of contrarious meats, I jump with them, many of our mystic cogitations procede; and even as fire maketh iron like itself, so the fiery inflammations of our liver or stomach transform our imaginations to their analogy and likeness.

No humour in general in our bodies overflowing or abounding, but the tips of our thoughts are dipped in his tincture. And as when a man is ready to drown, he takes hold of anything that is next him, so our fluttering thoughts, when we are drowned in deadly sleep, take hold and co-essence themselves with any overboiling humour which sourceth highest in our stomachs.

What heed then is there to be had of dreams that are no more but the confused giddy action of our brains, made drunk with the inundation of humours?

Just such-like impostures as is this art of exposition of dreams are the arts of physiognomy and palmistry, wherein who beareth most palm and praise is the palpablest fool and crepundio. Lives there any such slow, ice-brained, beef-witted gull, who by the rivelled bark or outward rind of a tree will take upon him to forespeak how long it shall stand, what mischances of worms, caterpillars, boughs breaking, frost bitings, cattle rubbing against, it shall have? As absurd is it, by the external branched seams or furrowed wrinkles in a man's face or hand, in particular or general to conjecture and foredoom of his fate.

According to every one's labour or exercise, the palm of his hand is written and plaited, and every day alters as he alters his employments or pastimes; wherefore well may we collect that he which hath a hand so brawned and interlined useth such-and-such toils or recreations; but for the mind or disposition, we can no more look into through it than we can into a looking glass through the wooden case thereof.

So also our faces, which sundry times with surfeits, grief, study or intemperance are most deformedly whelked and crumpled; there is no more to be gathered by their sharp embossed joiner's antique work or ragged overhangings or pitfalls but that they have been laid up in sloven's press, and with miscarriage and misgovernment are so fretted and galled.

My own experience is but small, yet thus much I can say by his warrantize that those fatal brands of physiognomy which condemn men for fools and for idiots, and on the other side for treacherous circumventers and false brothers, have in a hundred men I know been verified in the contrary.

So Socrates, the wisest man of Greece, was censured by a wrinkle-wizard for the lumpishest blockhead that ever went on two legs; whom though the philosopher in pity vouchsafed with a nice distinction of art and nature to raise and recover, when he was utterly confounded with a hiss and a laughter, yet sure his insolent simplicity might lawfully have sued out his patent of exemption, for he was a forlorn creature, both in discretion and wit-craft.

Will you have the sum of all: some subtle humourist, to feed fantastic heads with innovations and novelties, first invented this trifling childish glose upon dreams and physiognomy; wherein he strove only to boast himself of a pregnant probable conceit beyond philosophy or truth.

Let but any man who is most conversant in the superstition of dreams reckon me one that hath happened just, and I'll set down a hundred out of histories that have perished to foolery.

To come to late days. Lewis the xj. dreamt that he swam in blood on the top of the Alps, which one Father Robert, a holy hermit of his time, interpreted to be present death in his next wars against Italy, though he lived and prospered in all his enterprises a long while after.

So Charles the Fifth, sailing to the siege of Tunis, dreamt that the City met him on the sea like an Argosy, and over-whelmed his whole navy; when by Cornelius Agrippa, the great conjurer, who went along with him, it was expounded to be the overthrow of that famous expedition. And thereupon Agrippa offered the Emperor, if it pleased him to blow up the City by art magic in the air before his eyes without any farther jeopardy of war or beseiging. The Emperor utterly refused it and said since it was God's wars against an infidel, he would never borrow aid of the devil.

Some have memorized that Agrippa seeing his counsel in that case rejected, and that the Emperor, notwithstanding his unfortunate presage, was prosperous and successful, within few days after died frantic and desperate.

Alphonso, King of Naples, in like case, before the rumour of the French King's coming into Italy, had a vision in the night presented unto him of Aeneas' ghost having Turnus in chase, and Juno Pronuba coming betwixt them, and parting them; whereby he guessed that by marriage their jarring kingdoms should be united. But far otherwise it fell out, for the French King came indeed and he was driven thereby into such a melancholy ecstasy that he thought the very fowls of the air would snatch his crown from him, and no bough or arbour that

35

overshadowed him but enclosed him and took him prisoner, and that not so much but the stones of the street sought to justle him out of his throne.

These examples I allege, to prove there is no certainty in dreams, and that they are but according to our devisings and meditations in the daytime.

I confess the saints and martyrs of the Primitive Church had unfallible dreams fore-running their ends, as Policarpus and other; but those especially proceeded from heaven and not from any vaporous dreggy parts of our blood or our brains.

For this cause the Turks banish learning from amongst them, because it is every day setting men together by the ears, moving strange contentions and alterations, and making his professors faint-hearted and effeminate. Much more requisite were it that out of our civil Christian commonwealths we severely banish and exterminate those fabulous commentaries on toyish fantasies which fear-benumb and effeminate the hearts of the stoutest, cause a man without any ground to be jealous of his own friends and his kinsfolks, and withdraw him from the search and insight into more excellent things, to stand all his whole life sifting and winnowing dry rubbish chaff, whose best bottom quintescence proves in the end but sandy gravel and cockle.

Molestations and cares enough the ordinary course of our life tithes of his own accord unto us, though we seek not a knot in a bulrush, or stuff not our night-pillows with thistles to increase our disturbance.

In our sleep we are aghasted and terrified with the disordered skirmishing and conflicting of our sensitive faculties. Yet with this terror and aghastment cannot we rest ourselves satisfied, but we must pursue and hunt after a further fear in the recordation and too busy examining our pains over-passed.

Dreams in my mind if they have any premonstrances in them, the preparative fear of that they so premonstrate and denounce is far worse than the mischief itself by them denounced and premonstrated.

So there is no long sickness but is worse than death, for death is but a blow and away, whereas sickness is like a Chancery suit, which hangs two or three year ere it can come to a judgment.

Oh, a consumption is worse than a *Capias ad Ligatum*: to nothing can I compare it better than to a reprieve after a man is condemned, or to a boy with his hose about his heels, ready to be whipped, to whom his master stands preaching a long time all law and no gospel ere he proceed to execution. Or rather it is as a man should be roasted to death and melt away by little and little, whiles physicians like cooks stand stuffing him out with herbs and basting him with this oil and that syrup.

I am of the opinion that to be famished to death is far better, for his pain in seven or eight days is at an end, whereas he that is in a consumption continues languishing many years ere death have mercy on him.

The next plague and the nearest that I know in affinity

to a consumption is long depending hope frivolously defeated, than which there is no greater misery on earth, and so *per consequens* no men in earth more miserable than courtiers. It is a cowardly fear that is not resolute enough to despair. It is like a poor hunger-starved wretch at sea, who still in expectation of a good voyage endures more miseries than Job. He that writes this can tell, for he hath never had good voyage in his life but one, and that was to a fortunate blessed island near those pinacle rocks called the Needles. Oh, it is a purified continent, and a fertile plot fit to seat another paradise, where, or in no place, the image of the ancient hospitality is to be found.

While I live I will praise it and extol it for the true magnificence and continued honourable bounty that I saw there.

Far unworthy am I to spend the least breath of commendation in the extolling so delightful and pleasant a Tempe, or once to consecrate my ink with the excellent mention of the thrice-noble and illustrious chieftain under whom it is flourishingly governed.

That rare ornament of our country, learned Master Camden, whose desertful name is universally admired throughout Christendom, in the last re-polished edition of his *Britannia* hath most elaborate and exactly described the sovereign plenteous situation of that isle, as also the inestimable happiness it inherits, it being patronized and carefully protected by so heroical and courageous a commander.

Men that have never tasted that full spring of his liberality, wherewith, in my most forsaken extremities, right graciously he hath deigned to revive and refresh me, may rashly, at first sight, implead me of flattery and not esteem these my fervent terms as the necessary repayment of due debt, but words idly begotten with good looks, and in an over-joyed humour of vain hope slipped from me by chance; but therein they shall show themselves too uncivil injurious, both to my devoted observant duty and the condign dear purchased merit of his glory.

Too base a ground is this, whereon to embroider the rich story of his eternal renown; some longer-lived tractate I reserve for the full blaze of his virtues, which here only in the sparks I decipher. Many embers of encumbrances have I at this time, which forbid the bright flame of my zeal to mount aloft as it would. Perforce I must break from it, since other turbulent cares sit as now at the stern of my invention. Thus I conclude with this chance-medley parenthesis, that whatsoever minutes' intermission I have of calmed content, or least respite to call my wits together, principal and immediate proceedeth from him.

Through him my tender wainscot study door is delivered from much assault and battery. Through him I look into and am looked on in the world, from whence otherwise I were a wretched banished exile. Through him all my good, as by a conduit head, is conveyed unto me; and to him all my endeavours, like rivers, shall pay tribute as to the ocean.

Did Ovid entitle Carus, a nobleman of Rome, the only constant friend he had, in his ungrateful extrusion among the Getes, and writ to him thus:

Qui quod es id vere Care vocaris?

and in another elegy:

O mihi post nullos Care memorande sodales. *

Much more may I acknowledge all redundant prostrate vassalage to the royal descended family of the Careys, but for whom my spirit long ere this had expired, and my pen served as a poniard to gall my own heart.

Why do I use so much circumstance, and in a stream on which none but gnats and flies do swim sound Fame's trumpet like Triton to call a number of foolish skiffs and light cock-boats to parley?

Fear, if I be not deceived, was the last pertinent matter I had under my displing, from which I fear I have strayed beyond my limits; and yet fear hath no limits, for to hell and beyond hell it sinks down and penetrates.

But this was my position, that the fear of any expected evil is worse than the evil itself, which by divers comparisons I confirmed.

---

* 'After all my companions are gone, I will remember you, oh Carus.'

Now to visions and apparitions again, as fast as I can trudge.

The glasses of our sight, in the night, are like the prospective glasses one Hostius made in Rome, which represented the images of things far greater than they were. Each mote in the dark they make a monster, and every slight glimmering a giant.

A solitary man in his bed is like a poor bed-red lazar lying by the highway-side unto whose displayed wounds and sores a number of stinging flies do swarm for pastance and beverage. His naked wounds are his inward heart-griping woes, the wasps and flies his idle wandering thoughts; who to that secret smarting pain he hath already do add a further sting of impatience and new-lance his sleeping griefs and vexations.

Questionless, this is an unrefutable consequence, that the man who is mocked of his fortune, he that hath consumed his brains to compass prosperity and meets with no countervailment in her likeness, but hedge wine and lean mutton and peradventure some half-eyed good looks that can hardly be discerned from winking; this poor piteous perplexed miscreant either finally despairs, or like a lank frost-bitten plant loseth his vigour or spirit by little and little; any terror, the least illusion in the earth, is a Cacodaemon unto him. His soul hath left his body; for why, it is flying after these airy incorporate courtly promises, and glittering painted allurements, which when they vanish to nothing, it likewise vanisheth with them.

Excessive joy no less hath his defective and joyless operations, the spleen into water it melteth; so that except it be some momentary bubbles of mirth, nothing it yields but a cloying surfeit of repentance.

Divers instances have we of men whom too much sudden content and over-ravished delight hath brought untimely to their graves.

Four or five I have read of, whom the very extremity of laughter hath bereft of their lives; whereby I gather that even such another pernicious sweet, superfluous mirth is to the sense as a surfeit of honey to a man's stomach, than the which there is nothing more dangerous.

Be it as dangerous as it will, it cannot but be an easy kind of death. It is like one that is stung with an aspis, who in the midst of his pain falls delighted asleep, and in that suavity of slumber surrenders the ghost; whereas he whom grief undertakes to bring to his end, hath his heart gnawen in sunder by little and little with vultures, like Prometheus.

But this is nothing, you will object, to our journey's end of apparitions. Yes, altogether; for of the overswelling superabundance of joy and grief we frame to ourselves most of our melancholy dreams and visions.

There is an old philosophical common proverb, *Unusquisque fingit fortunam sibi*: everyone shapes his own fortune as he lists. More aptly may it be said: everyone shapes his own fears and fancies as he list.

In all points our brains are like the firmament, and

exhale in every respect the like gross mistempered vapours and meteors: of the more foeculent combustible airy matter whereof, affrighting forms and monstrous images innumerable are created, but of the slimy unwieldier drossy part, dull melancholy or drowsiness.

And as the firmament is still moving and working, so uncessant is the wheeling and rolling on of our brains, which every hour are tempering some new piece of prodigy or other, and turmoiling, mixing and changing the course of our thoughts.

I write not this for that I think there are no true apparitions or prodigies, but to show how easily we may be flouted if we take not great heed with our own antique suppositions. I will tell you a strange tale tending to this nature; whether of true melancholy or true apparition, I will not take upon me to determine.

It was my chance in February last to be in the country some threescore mile off from London, where a gentleman of good worship and credit falling sick, the very second day of his lying down he pretended to have miraculous waking visions, which before I enter to describe, thus much I will inform ye by the way, that at the reporting of them he was in perfect memory, nor had sickness yet so tyrannized over him to make his tongue grow idle. A wise, grave, sensible man he was ever reputed, and so approved himself in all his actions in his life-time. This which I deliver, with many preparative protestations, to a great man of this land he confidently avouched. Believe it or condemn it as you shall see cause, for I leave it to be censured indifferently.

The first day of his distemperature, he visibly saw, as he affirmed, all his chamber hung with silken nets and silver hooks, the devil, as it should seem, coming thither a-fishing. Whereupon, every *Pater-Noster*-while, he looked whether in the nets he should be entangled, or with the hooks ensnared. With the nets he feared to be strangled or smothered, and with the hooks to have his throat scratched out and his flesh rent and mangled. At length, he knew not how, they suddenly vanished and the whole chamber was cleared. Next a company of lusty sailors, every one a shirker or a swaggerer at the least, having made a brave voyage, came carousing and quaffing in large silver cans to his health. Fellows they were that had good big pop mouths to cry 'port, ahelm, Saint George', and knew as well as the best what belongs to haling of bolings yare and falling on the starboard buttock.

But to the issue of my tale. Their drunken proffers he utterly put by, and said he highly scorned and detested both them and their hellish disguisings; which notwithstanding, they tossed their cups to the skies, and reeled and staggered up and down the room like a ship shaking in the wind.

After all they danced lusty gallant and a drunken Danish lavalto or two, and so departed. For the third course, rushed in a number of stately devils, bringing in boisterous chests of massy treasure betwixt them. As brave they were as Turkish janissaries, having their apparel all powdered with gold and pearl, and their arms as it were bemailed with rich chains and bracelets, but faces far blacker than any ball of tobacco, great glaring eyes that had whole shelves of Kentish oysters in them, and terrible wide mouths, whereof not one of them but would well have made a case for Molenax' great globe of the world.

These lovely youths and full of favour, having stalked up and down the just measures of a sinkapace, opened one of the principal chests they brought, and out of it plucked a princely royal tent, whose empearled shining canopy they quickly advanced on high, and with all artificial magnificence adorned like a state; which performed, pompous Lucifer entered, imitating in goodly stature the huge picture of Laocoon at Rome, who sent unto him a gallant ambassador, signifying thus much, that if he would serve him, he should have all the rich treasure that he saw there, or any further wealth he would desire.

The gentleman returned this mild answer, that he knew not what he was, whether an angel or a wicked fiend, and if an angel, he was but his fellow servant, and no otherwise to be served or regarded; if a fiend, or a devil, he had nothing to do with him, for God had exalted and redeemed him above his desperate outcast condition, and a strong faith he had to defy and withstand all his juggling temptations. Having uttered these words, all the whole train of them invisibly avoided, and he never set eye on them after.

Then did there, for the third pageant, present themselves unto him an inveigling troop of naked virgins,
thrice more amiable and beautiful than the bright vestals
that brought in Augustus' Testament to the Senate after
his decease; but no vestal-like ornament had they about
them, for from top to toe bare despoiled they were, except
some one or two of them that ware masks before their
faces, and had transparent azured lawn veils before the
chief jewel-houses of their honours.

Such goodly lustful bonarobaes they were, by his
report, as if any sharp-eyed painter had been there to
peruse them, he might have learned to exceed divine
Michael Angelo in the true bosk of a naked, or curious
Tuns in quick life, whom the great masters of that art do
term the sprightly old man.

Their hair they ware loose unrolled about their shoulders, whose dangling amber trammels reaching down
beneath their knees seemed to drop balm on their deli-
cious bodies, and ever as they moved to and fro, with
their light windy wavings, wantonly to correct their
exquisite mistresses.

Their dainty feet in their tender birdlike trippings
enamelled, as it were, the dusty ground; and their odor-
iferous breath more perfumed the air than ordnance
would that is charged with amomum, musk, civet and
ambergreece.

But to leave amplifications and proceed. Those sweet
bewitching naked maids, having majestically paced about

the chamber, to the end their natural unshelled shining mother pearl proportions might be more imprintingly apprehended, close to his bedside modestly blushing they approached, and made impudent proffer unto him of their lascivious embraces. He, obstinately bent to withstand these their sinful allurements, no less than the former, bad them go seek entertainment of hotter bloods, for he had not to satisfy them. A cold comfort was this to poor wenches no better clothed, yet they hearing what to trust to, very sorrowfully retired and shrunk away.

Lo, in the fourth act there sallied out a grave assembly of sober-attired matrons, much like the virgins of Mary Magdalen's order in Rome, which vow never to see man, or the chaste daughters of Saint Philip.

With no incontinent courtesy did they greet him, but told him if he thought good they would pray for him.

Thereupon, from the beginning to the ending he unfolded unto them how he had been mightily haunted with wicked illusions of late, but nevertheless, if he could be persuaded that they were angels or saints, their invocations could not hurt him; yea, he would add his desire to their requests to make their prayers more penetrably enforcing.

Without further parley, upon their knees they fell most devoutly and for half-an-hour never ceased extensively to intercessionate GOD for his speedy recovery.

Rising up again on the right hand of his bed, there appeared a clear light, and with that he might perceive a

47

naked slender foot offering to steal betwixt the sheets in to him.

At which instant, entered a messenger from a knight of great honour thereabouts, who sent him a most precious extract quintessence to drink; which no sooner he tasted, but he thought he saw all the fore-named interluders at once hand-over-head leap, plunge and drown themselves in puddles and ditches hard by, and he felt perfect ease.

But long it lasted not with him, for within four hours after, having not fully settled his estate in order, he grew to trifling dotage, and raving died within two days following.

God is my witness, in all this relation I borrow no essential part from stretched-out invention, nor have I one jot abused my informations; only for the recreation of my readers, whom loath to tire with a coarse home-spun tale that should dull them worse than Holland cheese, here and there I welt and gard it with allusive exornations and comparisons; and yet methinks it comes off too gouty and lumbering.

Be it as it will, it is like to have no more allowance of English for me. If the world will give it any allowance of truth, so it is. For then I hope my excuse is already lawfully customed and authorized, since Truth is ever drawn and painted naked, and I have lent her but a leathern patched cloak at most to keep her from the cold; that is, that she come not off too lamely and coldly.

Upon the accidental occasion of this dream or

apparition (call or miscall it what you will, for it is yours as freely as any waste paper that ever you had in your lives) was this pamphlet (no bigger than an old preface) speedily botched up and compiled.

Are there any doubts which remain in your mind undigested, as touching this incredible narration I have unfolded? Well, doubt you not, but I am mild and tractable and will resolve you in what I may.

First, the house where this gentleman dwelt stood in a low marish ground, almost as rotten a climate as the Low Countries, where their misty air is as thick as mould butter, and the dew lies like frothy barm on the ground. It was noted over and besides to have been an unlucky house to all his predecessors, situate in a quarter not altogether exempted from witches. The abrupt falling into his sickness was suspicious, proceeding from no apparent surfeit or misdiet. The outrageous tyranny of it in so short a time bred thrice more admiration and wonder, and his sudden death incontinent ensuing upon that his disclosed dream or vision, might seem some probable reason to confirm it, since none have such palpable dreams or visions but die presently after.

The like to this was Master Alington's vision in the beginning of Her Majesty's reign; than the which there is nothing more ordinarily bruited. Through Greek and Roman commonplaces to this purport I could run, if I were disposed to vaunt myself like a ridiculous pedant of deep reading in Fulgosius, Licosthenes and Valerius.

Go no further than the Court, and they will tell you of a mighty worthy man of this land, who riding in his coach from London to his house was all the way haunted with a couple of hogs, who followed him close, and do what his men could, they might not drive them from him. Wherefore at night he caused them to be shut up in a barn and commanded milk to be given them; the barn door was locked, and the key safely kept, yet were they gone by morning, and no man knew how.

A number of men there be yet living who have been haunted by their wives after their death about forswearing themselves and undoing their children of whom they promised to be careful fathers; whereof I can gather no reason but this, that women are born to torment a man both alive and dead.

I have heard of others likewise, that besides these night-terrors, have been, for whole months together, whithersoever they went or rid, pursued by weasels and rats, and oftentimes with squirrels and hares, that in the travelling of three hundred mile have still waited on their horse heels.

But those are only the exploits and stratagems of witches, which may well astonish a little at first sight, but if a man have the least heart or spirit to withstand one fierce blast of their bravadoes, he shall see them shrink faster than northern cloth, and outstrip time in dastardly flight.

Fie, fie, was ever poor fellow so far benighted in an old wive's tale of devils and urchins! Out upon it, I am weary of it, for it hath caused such a thick fulsome serena to descend on my brain that now my pen makes blots as broad as a furred stomacher, and my muse inspires me to put out my candle and go to bed; and yet I will not neither, till, after all these nights' revels I have solemnly bid you goodnight, as much to say as tell you how you shall have a good night, and sleep quietly without affrightment and annoyance.

First and foremost, drink moderately, and dice and drab not away your money prodigally and then foreswear yourselves to borrow more.

You that be poor men's children, know your own fathers; and though you can shift and cheat yourselves into good clothes here about town, yet bow your knees to their leathern bags and russet coats, that they may bless you from the ambition of Tyburn.

You that bear the name of soldiers and live basely swaggering in every ale-house, having no other exhibition but from harlots and strumpets, seek some new trade, and leave whoring and quarrelling, lest besides the nightly guilt of your own bankrout consciences, Bridewell or Newgate prove the end of your cavaliering.

You, whosoever or wheresoever you be, that live by spoiling and overreaching young gentlemen, and make but a sport to deride their simplicities to their undoing, to you the night at one time or other will prove terrible, except you forthwith think on restitution; or if you have not your night in this world, you will have it in hell.

You that are married and have wives of your own, and yet hold too near friendship with your neighbours', set up your rests that the night will be an ill neighbour to your rest and that you shall have as little peace of mind as the rest. Therefore was Troy burnt by night, because Paris by night prostituted Helena, and wrought such treason to Prince Menelaus.

You that are Machiavellian vain fools, and think it no wit or policy but to vow and protest what you never mean, that travel for nothing else but to learn the vices of other countries and disfigure the ill English faces that God hath given you with Tuscan glicks and apish tricks: the night is for you a black saunt or a matachine, except you presently turn and convert to the simplicity you were born to.

You that can cast a man into an Italian ague when you list, and imitate with your diet-drinks any disease or infirmity, the night likewise hath an infernal to act before ye.

Traitors that by night meet and consult how to walk in the day undiscovered, and think those words of Christ revealed and laid open: to you no less the night shall be as a night owl to vex and torment you.

And finally, on you judges and magistrates, if there be any amongst you that do wrest all the law into their own hands, by drawing and receiving every man's money into their hands, and making new golden laws of their own, which no prince nor parliament ever dreamed of; that look as just as Jehovah by day, enthronizing grave zeal and religion on the elevated whites of their eyes, when by night corrupt gifts and rewards rush in at their gates in whole armies, like northern carriers coming to their inn; that instead of their books turn over their bribes, for the deciding of causes, adjudging him the best right that brings the richest present unto them. If any such there be, I say, as in our Commonwealth I know none, but have read of in other states, let them look to have a number of unwelcome clients of their own accusing thoughts and imaginations that will betray them in the night to every idle fear and illusion.

Therefore are the terrors of the night more than of the day, because the sins of the night surmount the sins of the day.

By night-time came the Deluge over the face of the whole earth; by night-time Judas betrayed Christ, Tarquin ravished Lucretia.

When any poet would describe a horrible tragical accident, to add the more probability and credence unto it, he dismally beginneth to tell how it was dark night when it was done and cheerful daylight had quite abandoned the firmament.

Hence it is, that sin generally throughout the scripture is called the works of darkness; for never is the devil so busy as then, and then he thinks he may as well undiscovered walk abroad, as homicides and outlaws.

Had we no more religion than we might derive from

53

heathen fables, methinks those doleful quiristers of the night, the scritch-owl, the nightingale, and croaking frogs, might overawe us from any insolent transgression at that time. The first for her lavish blabbing of forbidden secrets, being for ever ordained to be a blab of ill-news and misfortune, still is crying out in our ears that we are mortal and must die. The second puts us in mind of the end and punishment of lust and ravishment. And the third and last, that we are but slime and mud, such as those watery creatures are bred of; and therefore why should we delight to add more to our slime and corruption, by extraordinary surfeits and drunkenness?

But these are nothing neither in comparison. For he whom in the day heaven cannot exhale, the night will never help; she only pleading for her old grandmother hell as well as the day for heaven.

Thus I shut up my treatise abruptly: that he who in the day doth not good works enough to answer the objections of the night, will hardly answer at the Day of Judgment.

1. BOCCACCIO · *Mrs Rosie and the Priest*
2. GERARD MANLEY HOPKINS · *As kingfishers catch fire*
3. *The Saga of Gunnlaug Serpent-tongue*
4. THOMAS DE QUINCEY · *On Murder Considered as One of the Fine Arts*
5. FRIEDRICH NIETZSCHE · *Aphorisms on Love and Hate*
6. JOHN RUSKIN · *Traffic*
7. PU SONGLING · *Wailing Ghosts*
8. JONATHAN SWIFT · *A Modest Proposal*
9. *Three Tang Dynasty Poets*
10. WALT WHITMAN · *On the Beach at Night Alone*
11. KENKŌ · *A Cup of Sake Beneath the Cherry Trees*
12. BALTASAR GRACIÁN · *How to Use Your Enemies*
13. JOHN KEATS · *The Eve of St Agnes*
14. THOMAS HARDY · *Woman much missed*
15. GUY DE MAUPASSANT · *Femme Fatale*
16. MARCO POLO · *Travels in the Land of Serpents and Pearls*
17. SUETONIUS · *Caligula*
18. APOLLONIUS OF RHODES · *Jason and Medea*
19. ROBERT LOUIS STEVENSON · *Olalla*
20. KARL MARX AND FRIEDRICH ENGELS · *The Communist Manifesto*
21. PETRONIUS · *Trimalchio's Feast*
22. JOHANN PETER HEBEL · *How a Ghastly Story Was Brought to Light by a Common or Garden Butcher's Dog*
23. HANS CHRISTIAN ANDERSEN · *The Tinder Box*
24. RUDYARD KIPLING · *The Gate of the Hundred Sorrows*
25. DANTE · *Circles of Hell*
26. HENRY MAYHEW · *Of Street Piemen*
27. HAFEZ · *The nightingales are drunk*
28. GEOFFREY CHAUCER · *The Wife of Bath*
29. MICHEL DE MONTAIGNE · *How We Weep and Laugh at the Same Thing*
30. THOMAS NASHE · *The Terrors of the Night*
31. EDGAR ALLAN POE · *The Tell-Tale Heart*
32. MARY KINGSLEY · *A Hippo Banquet*
33. JANE AUSTEN · *The Beautifull Cassandra*
34. ANTON CHEKHOV · *Gooseberries*
35. SAMUEL TAYLOR COLERIDGE · *Well, they are gone, and here must I remain*
36. JOHANN WOLFGANG VON GOETHE · *Sketchy, Doubtful, Incomplete Jottings*
37. CHARLES DICKENS · *The Great Winglebury Duel*
38. HERMAN MELVILLE · *The Maldive Shark*
39. ELIZABETH GASKELL · *The Old Nurse's Story*
40. NIKOLAY LESKOV · *The Steel Flea*

41. HONORÉ DE BALZAC · *The Atheist's Mass*
42. CHARLOTTE PERKINS GILMAN · *The Yellow Wall-Paper*
43. C.P. CAVAFY · *Remember, Body . . .*
44. FYODOR DOSTOEVSKY · *The Meek One*
45. GUSTAVE FLAUBERT · *A Simple Heart*
46. NIKOLAI GOGOL · *The Nose*
47. SAMUEL PEPYS · *The Great Fire of London*
48. EDITH WHARTON · *The Reckoning*
49. HENRY JAMES · *The Figure in the Carpet*
50. WILFRED OWEN · *Anthem For Doomed Youth*
51. WOLFGANG AMADEUS MOZART · *My Dearest Father*
52. PLATO · *Socrates' Defence*
53. CHRISTINA ROSSETTI · *Goblin Market*
54. *Sindbad the Sailor*
55. SOPHOCLES · *Antigone*
56. RYŪNOSUKE AKUTAGAWA · *The Life of a Stupid Man*
57. LEO TOLSTOY · *How Much Land Does A Man Need?*
58. GIORGIO VASARI · *Leonardo da Vinci*
59. OSCAR WILDE · *Lord Arthur Savile's Crime*
60. SHEN FU · *The Old Man of the Moon*
61. AESOP · *The Dolphins, the Whales and the Gudgeon*
62. MATSUO BASHŌ · *Lips too Chilled*
63. EMILY BRONTË · *The Night is Darkening Round Me*
64. JOSEPH CONRAD · *To-morrow*
65. RICHARD HAKLUYT · *The Voyage of Sir Francis Drake Around the Whole Globe*
66. KATE CHOPIN · *A Pair of Silk Stockings*
67. CHARLES DARWIN · *It was snowing butterflies*
68. BROTHERS GRIMM · *The Robber Bridegroom*
69. CATULLUS · *I Hate and I Love*
70. HOMER · *Circe and the Cyclops*
71. D. H. LAWRENCE · *Il Duro*
72. KATHERINE MANSFIELD · *Miss Brill*
73. OVID · *The Fall of Icarus*
74. SAPPHO · *Come Close*
75. IVAN TURGENEV · *Kasyan from the Beautiful Lands*
76. VIRGIL · *O Cruel Alexis*
77. H. G. WELLS · *A Slip under the Microscope*
78. HERODOTUS · *The Madness of Cambyses*
79. *Speaking of Siva*
80. *The Dhammapada*